Inflation 101

INFLATION 101: WHAT YOU NEED TO KNOW ABOUT INFLATION

By

John J. Morgan

Inflation 101

Copyright © by John J. Morgan 2022. All rights reserved.

Before this document is duplicated or reproduced in any manner, the publisher's consent must be gained. Therefore, the contents within can neither be stored electronically, transferred, nor kept in a database. Neither in Part nor full can the document be copied, scanned, faxed, or retained without approval from the publisher or creator.

Inflation 101

TABLE OF CONTENTS

INTRODUCTION 4
CHAPTER ONE 12
    Deflation 14
    What Is Hyperinflation? 15
    What is Stagflation? 16
CHAPTER TWO 17
    Demand-Pull Inflation 17
    Cost-Push Inflation 18
    How Is Inflation Measured? 18
    Consumer Price Index (CPI) 19
    Producer Price Index (PPI) 20
    Personal Consumption Expenditures Price Index (PCE)..20
    Inflation And The FED 21
CHAPTER THREE..22
    The Great Inflation (1965–1982).....................................22
    Investigations Into the Great Inflation 23
    The Motive: The Phillips Curve And The Pursuit Of Full Employment 24
    The Instrument: Bretton Woods' Collapse 27
    The Opportunity: Fiscal Imbalances, Energy Shortages, and Bad Data 29

The Conquest of Us Inflation: From High Inflation to
Inflation Targeting 31
CHAPTER FOUR.. 37
   NEGATIVE EFFECTS OF INFLATION 37
   POSITIVE EFFECTS OF INFLATION............................ 44
   HOW TO BEAT INFLATION 47
CHAPTER SIX 50
   CONCLUSION 50

Inflation 101

INTRODUCTION

We are at present, residing through the greatest inflation emergency since the 1980s. In those days inflation rates were going as high as 14 anyway throughout the previous 40 years inflation has been on a descending pattern and hasn't approached the pinnacles of the 80s that was obviously until 2021 when inflation rates began to soar currently were all feeling the spot of more exorbitant costs you're paying 10 more for food today than you were a year prior 32 something else for energy and 10 percent something else for carrier travel add in spiking rental costs rising house costs and the biggest retirement emergency in current history but we've got a few major difficulties since this emergency is profoundly influencing all of us I figured we could examine the reason why this emergency exists what's being finished to tackle it and how you can best set yourself up for the next few months sadly you don't have a ton of time to get ready worldwide national banks are wanting to make changes which haven't been seen for quite a long time which we'll examine so there's heaps of vulnerability for the future making it much more vital to be ready so the way that terrible is the inflation emergency 100 today would just get you 58 worth of food in 2000 all in all the buying force of the dollar has fallen by 42 in only 20 years how has this happened well the issue began during the extraordinary downturn somewhere in the

Inflation 101

range of 07 and 09. the breakdown of the U.S real estate market had unleashed devastation worldwide to keep the economy above water the U.S national bank also called the central bank chose to utilize an apparatus called quantitative facilitating or QE for absence of a superior clarification national banks can print cash out of nowhere quantitative facilitating includes national banks utilizing this cash to purchase bunches of monetary resources like government securities and home loan upheld protections without carefully describing the situation quantitative facilitating makes getting cash less expensive hence bringing about more cash coursing in the economy which supports spending it additionally has the optional impact of expanding how much cash put resources into the financial exchange yet favoring that later there have been multiple times beginning around 2008 where quantitative facilitating has been utilized by the fed here and here each time quantitative facilitating is utilized it downgrades the dollar in light of the fact that the fed printing new dollars debases dollars currently in presence as we can obviously see from the diagram the fed printed a crazy measure of cash in light of the worldwide pandemic to place this into setting in august 2008 the fed had around 900 billion bucks worth of resources on its monetary record as of writing this book. That figure is presently almost nine trillion bucks. A ten times increment basically the fed has decisively expanded the quantity of dollars in the economy by means of quantitative facilitating starting around 2008 and this has prompted huge interest for labor and products.

Inflation 101

The issue is that worldwide stockpile chains are broken the pandemic overwhelms existing inventory chains with one measurement taking note of that the typical compartment currently invests 20 more energy in the framework we had flooding levels of customer interest simultaneously as severe clandestine conventions which confined supply so what happens when you have an excessive number of dollars pursuing too couple of merchandise financial matters 101 lets us know that costs increment and that is precisely where our inflation is coming from today to exacerbate the situation the Russian intrusion of Ukraine as well as proceeded with severe testing methods in China are deteriorating what is going on you've no question felt the impacts of flooding product costs and this is to a great extent because of key stock channels being cut off in view of the conflict yet what's truly vital to comprehend is that it's not simply broken supply chains which are driving greater costs it's the interest for labor and products which is causing pressure so that welcomes us on to what's being finished to settle the inflation emergency most importantly the central bank halted their quantitative facilitating program in walk this was them reassessing the cash printer which has been running for the beyond two years and the impacts of this are now being felt the 10-year U.S depository yield is going to hit 3 a level which it hasn't came to beginning around 2018. this is huge in light of the fact that the 10-year yield is utilized as a benchmark while setting loan fees for contracts and different credits; the higher the yield, the higher getting costs become. I referenced toward

Inflation 101

the starting that worldwide national banks want to make changes that haven't been seen for quite a long time. These progressions will come through increasing financing costs. The government supports a compelling rate which is the loan fee that banks charge each other for acquiring or loaning cash has been basically zero since 2020, yet last month the fed expanded this rate by 0.25 percent, the first inflation in quite a while, and presently were taking a gander at an extra increment of 0.5 percent in May which would be the greatest inflation in more than 20 years these increments will probably go on all through the remainder of 2022.

The objective here is to build the general expense of getting consequently decreasing how much money circling in the economy thusly diminishing interest for labor and products this is a cycle of a situation with two sides from one viewpoint inflation certainly should be tended to as the typical cost for many everyday items is rapidly spiraling crazy anyway then again lodging moderateness will just deteriorate with these progressions 30-year fixed-rate contract rates in the us have typically begun to skyrocket to the most significant levels in 11 years with the progressions presented by the fed and with house costs having expanded by almost 20% in one year homeownership is seeming to be an unrealistic fantasy for the more youthful ages the inquiry is whether the federal authorities strategy changes will bring about a downturn genuinely we don't understand what the full effect of the progressions will be nevertheless there certainly will be ramifications just like the

Inflation 101

idea of focal banking expanding the expense of getting assists the fed with easing back request yet the outcomes of that are more slow financial development and logical higher joblessness yet what the fed truly needs to stay away from is stagflation is a terrible mix of excessive costs high joblessness and low monetary result reporters like Beam Dalio accept that a time of stagflation is coming for the U.S very much like the way that it did during the 1970s thought being that the federal authorities loan fee changes won't be sufficient to check inflation yet will be sufficient to slow financial development and increment joblessness obviously the inflation emergency is really convoluted and there are a bunch of vulnerabilities which make it hard to estimate what way the next few months will go the positions market is likewise assuming a significant part in the inflation were finding in February there were 11.3 million employment opportunities in the us representatives have huge bartering influence right now fundamentally because of the extraordinary renunciation and the cry for laborers we realize that individuals are changing position and getting compensated a lot more significant compensations to battle inflation the issue is that inflation is an unavoidable outcome paying your laborers more cash to represent inflation thus causes inflation as higher business costs are given to the clients who are presently following through on greater expenses in like manner assuming customers are anticipating that costs should be higher in the future they'll basically purchase more merchandise today which thus increments future costs the inflation emergency has tested

Inflation 101

the maintainability of our ongoing money related frameworks and brings up the issue of whether there's potential in moving to a computerized cash Joe Biden as of late marked a chief request on digital forms of money where he asked the equity division and the depository to explore the potential for making a national bank advanced money or CBDC and we realize that this is likewise something that the fed has investigated a CBDC would go about as a computerized dollar gave and supported by the fed most as of late U.S depository secretary Janet Yellen went on record saying that a CBDC could without a doubt turn into a confided in type of cash tantamount to actual money yet she additionally noticed that such change would require numerous years to become an integral factor because of the intricacies of the interaction honestly its still too soon to understand which job computerized monetary forms will play in our social orders from here on out yet what's most fascinating is the way digital forms of money and CBDCs will coincide close by one another with cryptos being decentralized and CBDC as yet staying concentrated you may be considering what the inflation emergency will mean for your ventures going ahead and how you ought to be safeguarding yourself actually increasing loan fees and blurring support from national banks will hurt the financial exchange the s p 500 is down just about 10 since the finish of walk that is truly for three reasons the main explanation is the way stock costs are determined the cost of any stock on the financial exchange is determined as the business sectors assumptions for future incomes limited back to the current day

Inflation 101

the higher loan fees go the bigger the markdown will be which brings about a fall in stock costs in addition to higher financing costs can slow result for organizations converting into lower future incomes and profit the subsequent explanation is that there's less cash going into the market the justification for why financing costs ascend in any case is to fix the stockpile of cash so normally there will be less cash accessible to put resources into stocks the third explanation is that loan costs on securities are expanding and in light of the fact that securities are generally safer ventures than stocks financial backers leave the securities exchange for the more significant yields presented by securities the best thing you can do right presently is to abstain from overspending on non-esteem adding things when the cost for many everyday items is going up its precisely the same thing as getting a compensation sliced so you really want to regard your spending as though you had gotten a compensation cut focus on the essential costs and give a valiant effort to reside inside your means and save and contribute as long as possible.

Indeed it has never been more essential to have a secret stash yet its similarly never been more vital to be on top of your speculations for the future this is the situation with regards to long haul effective financial planning you must have the option to adjust to both the great times and the terrible times and its consistently similar in 10 15 years individuals think back and say gracious I wish I hadn't sold or goodness I wish I continued financial planning during that time recall whether you missed the best 10 days of the securities exchange throughout recent

Inflation 101

years your profit from venture throughout that time span will be sliced down the middle at the end of the day you must be not fooling around recollect that regardless of how you decide to manage your money insofar as its sitting in a ledger thus lengthy as inflation is high you're losing cash so that pretty much wraps up the inflation emergency and definitely it's a precarious circumstance look its exceptionally simple to become involved with the despair and destruction of everything when as a general rule the proper thing to do is to be cost cognizant and to constantly recollect the nuts and bolts.

Inflation 101

CHAPTER ONE

WHAT IS INFLATION ?

In the field of economics, inflation refers to an overall rise in the cost of goods and services throughout a nation. Each unit of currency may purchase fewer products and services when the general price level rises; hence, inflation is associated with a decline in the purchasing power of money. Deflation, a continuous drop in the general level of prices for goods and services, is the reverse of inflation. The annualized percentage change in a general price index, or inflation rate, is the most widely used indicator of inflation. The consumer price index (CPI) is frequently employed for this purpose because price increases are not uniform across the board. In the United States, wages are also calculated using the employment cost index.

When prices increase throughout the economy, your money has less buying power and inflation results. For instance, the average price of a cinema ticket in 1980 was $2.89. The average cost of a movie ticket increased to $9.16 by 2019. A $10 dollar from 1980 would buy two fewer movie tickets in 2019 than it did nearly four decades earlier if you had saved it.

Inflation 101

However, don't conceive of inflation as simply increasing costs for a single good or service. A country's overall economy, as well as a sector or industry like the automotive or energy industries, may ultimately experience inflation.

The Consumer Price Index (CPI), Producer Price Index (PPI), and Personal Consumption Expenditures Price Index (PCE), which all use different measures to track the change in prices consumers pay and producers receive in industries across the entire American economy, are the three main measures of U.S. inflation.

Although it can be discouraging to realize that your money is depreciating, most economists view a tiny amount of inflation as a positive indicator of a robust economy. A moderate inflation rate encourages you to invest or use your money now rather than stowing it away and watching it lose value.

If inflation is let to spiral out of control and increase significantly, it can become a damaging force for an economy. Unchecked inflation may destroy a nation's economy, as Venezuela experienced in 2018 when its inflation rate reached over 1,000,000% per month, leading to the collapse of the economy and the exodus of countless inhabitants.

Inflation 101

Deflation

Deflation is a decrease in prices across all economic sectors or the overall economy. The ability to purchase more for less money tomorrow may seem appealing, but experts caution that deflation can be even more harmful to an economy than unrestrained inflation.

When deflation sets in, buyers put off current purchases in anticipation of more significant price drops in the future. Deflation can reduce or even stop economic growth if it is allowed to continue, which would destroy wages and paralyze an economy.

When inflation isn't kept in check, it's commonly known as hyperinflation or stagflation. These terms describe out-of-control inflation that cripples consumers' purchasing power and economies.

What Is Hyperinflation?

When inflation increases quickly and a country's currency value falls quickly, this is known as hyperinflation. According to economists, hyperinflation occurs when monthly price increases are at least 50%. Hyperinflation has occasionally occurred in the past during civil unrest, war, or when regimes have been overthrown, effectively devaluing money.

Inflation 101

In Germany's Weimar Republic in the early 1920s, hyperinflation may have its best-known instance. Each month, prices increased by tens of thousands of percent, severely harming the German economy.

What is Stagflation?

Stagflation happens when inflation remains high while a country's economy stagnates and unemployment rises. Consumer demand typically declines as people manage their expenditures more carefully when unemployment rises. Your purchasing power is rebalanced as a result of the decline in demand, which lowers prices.

However, when stagflation takes place, prices stay high even while consumer spending falls, making it more and more expensive to purchase the same products. We don't need to look outside of the country for instances, since the United States suffered stagflation in the middle to late 1970s due to high prices brought on by OPEC oil embargoes, which increased inflation even while recessionary conditions reduced GDP and raised unemployment.

CHAPTER TWO

WHAT CAUSES INFLATION?

The gradually rising prices associated with inflation can be caused two main ways: demand-pull inflation and cost-push inflation. Both come back to the fundamental economic principles of supply and demand.

Demand-Pull Inflation

Demand-pull When supply of goods or services is constant but demand is rising, prices will rise. There are several ways to generate demand-pull inflation. In a strong economy, both individuals and businesses see rising profits. Consumers now have more purchasing power than they did previously, which increases competition for already-existing commodities and drives up prices even while businesses try to increase output. Smaller-scale abrupt product popularity spikes can lead to demand-pull inflation.

For instance, with the commencement of the coronavirus pandemic, the rise in interest in indoor, isolating activities and the much-awaited release of Animal Crossing: New Leaf: The

Inflation 101

cost of the Nintendo Switch game console has doubled on some secondary marketplaces, according to New Horizons. Because Nintendo was unable to boost production as a result of factory production halts brought on by Covid-19, it was unable to increase its supply in order to satisfy growing consumer demand, which led to steadily rising costs.

Cost-Push Inflation

Cost-push inflation occurs when the supply of goods or services is restricted in any way but demand is constant, prices will rise. The ability of businesses to create enough of a particular commodity to meet consumer demand is typically hampered by some form of external catastrophe, such as a natural disaster. Inflation results from them being able to raise prices as a result.

Consider the price of oil, for instance. To fill up your car, you and pretty much everyone else needs a particular quantity of gas. Gas prices increase when international agreements or natural catastrophes significantly cut the oil supply because demand is essentially stable even as supply declines.

How Is Inflation Measured?

The CPI, PPI, and PCE indices are used to calculate the U.S. inflation rate. Economists must take into account these several

Inflation 101

indexes in order to provide a complete picture of the rate of inflation because no single index can fully capture the spectrum of price changes in the US economy.

The following is the fundamental formula to determine the inflation rate:

(Current Price − Former Price)/Former Price

Consumer Price Index (CPI)

The CPI is determined monthly by the U.S. Bureau of Labor Statistics using changes in the prices consumers pay for goods and services. The CPI employs a "basket of goods" methodology, which means that it monitors changes in the prices of eight major consumer goods categories: food and drink, housing, clothing, transportation, education and communication, recreation, health care, and miscellaneous goods and services.

The CPI is frequently used as the standard for gauging inflation in the US. Because it is used to determine cost-of-living adjustments for Social Security benefits and many corporations' yearly raises, the CPI is particularly significant. The rates on some inflation-protected assets, such as Treasury Inflation-Protected Securities, are also adjusted using this method (TIPS).

Inflation 101

Producer Price Index (PPI)

PPI, which is also released by the Bureau of Labor Statistics, keeps track of changes in the prices that businesses are paid each month for the goods and services they offer. Costs can increase when producers deal with rising tariffs, greater fuel costs to transport their goods, or other problems like the effects of a protracted pandemic or natural changes like an increase in storms, wildfires, or flooding.

PPI is a crucial component in commercial contracts. Businesses commonly use the PPI to automatically alter the rate they pay for raw products and services over time when they enter into long-term contracts with suppliers. Otherwise, suppliers would commit themselves to multiyear agreements at prices that would eventually result in a loss of purchasing power.

Personal Consumption Expenditures Price Index (PCE)

PCE, which is released by the Bureau of Economic Analysis, keeps track of how much consumers spend on goods and services. Compared to the CPI, this index takes a wider variety of consumer spending into account, including healthcare expenses. Instead of confining data to a predetermined set of commodities, it also changes the basket of goods it uses for computations based on what consumers are actually spending money on each month.

Inflation 101

Because PCE is the Federal Reserve's favored method of measuring inflation for making monetary policy decisions, it is particularly significant.

Inflation And The FED

The U.S.'s central bank is called the Federal Reserve, and like central banks everywhere else, its job is to keep inflation at a steady level. The Federal Open Markets Committee (FOMC) has established that for the best employment and price stability, an inflation rate of about 2% is ideal.

With this level of inflation, the FOMC has the ability to reduce interest rates, which lowers the cost of borrowing and helps increase demand during economic downturns. Lower interest rates make borrowing money more affordable for consumers and businesses, so boosting the economy. As a result of lower interest rates, people get less income on their savings, which encourages them to spend. However, all of this additional demand may raise inflation.

CHAPTER THREE

THE GREATEST INFLATION IN U.S HISTORY

The Great Inflation (1965–1982)

The second part of the twentieth century's macroeconomic history was characterized by The Great Inflation. It lasted from 1965 to 1982 and caused economists to reevaluate the Fed's and other central banks' monetary policies.

The second half of the 20th century's most significant macroeconomic event was The Great Inflation. The post-World War II global monetary system was abandoned during that time, and there were four economic downturns, two major energy shortages, and the first-ever application of wage and price restrictions in peacetime. It was "the worst failure of American macroeconomic policy in the postwar century," according to one well-known economist (Siegel 1994).

However, that failure also resulted in a fundamental shift in macroeconomic theory, which ultimately led to the rules that now direct the monetary policies of the Federal Reserve and other central banks across the world. If the Great Inflation was a

Inflation 101

result of a serious flaw in American macroeconomic policy, then defeating it should be celebrated as a victory.

Investigations Into the Great Inflation

Inflation in 1964 was somewhat higher than 1% each year. Over the six years prior, it had resided in this area. Midway through the 1960s, inflation started to increase and peaked in 1980 at over 14 percent. In the latter half of the 1980s, it gradually decreased to an average of barely 3.5 percent.

While there is some disagreement among economists over the relative weight of the causes that spurred and sustained inflation for more than a decade, there is minimal disagreement regarding its origin. The Federal Reserve policies that allowed for an excessive increase in the supply of money were the cause of the Great Inflation.

It will be helpful to explain the story in three separate but connected parts so that the episode of very terrible policy, and monetary policy in particular, can be understood. This is a kind of forensic study that looks at the reason, means, and chance for the Great Inflation to happen.

Inflation 101

The Motive: The Phillips Curve And The Pursuit Of Full Employment

The first section of the narrative, which explains the cause of the Great Inflation, began soon after the Great Depression, an earlier but no less revolutionary time for macroeconomic theory and practice. Following the end of World War II, Congress focused on measures it anticipated would encourage more economic stability. The Employment Act of 1946 stands out among the new laws the most. The act, among other things, mandated tighter coordination between monetary and fiscal policy and stated that it was the duty of the federal government "to encourage maximum employment, production, and purchasing power. The Federal Reserve's current dual mandate to "maintain long run expansion of the monetary and credit aggregates...so as to effectively achieve the goals of maximum employment, stable prices, and moderate long-term interest rates" is fundamentally derived from this statute (Steelman 2011).

Inflation 101

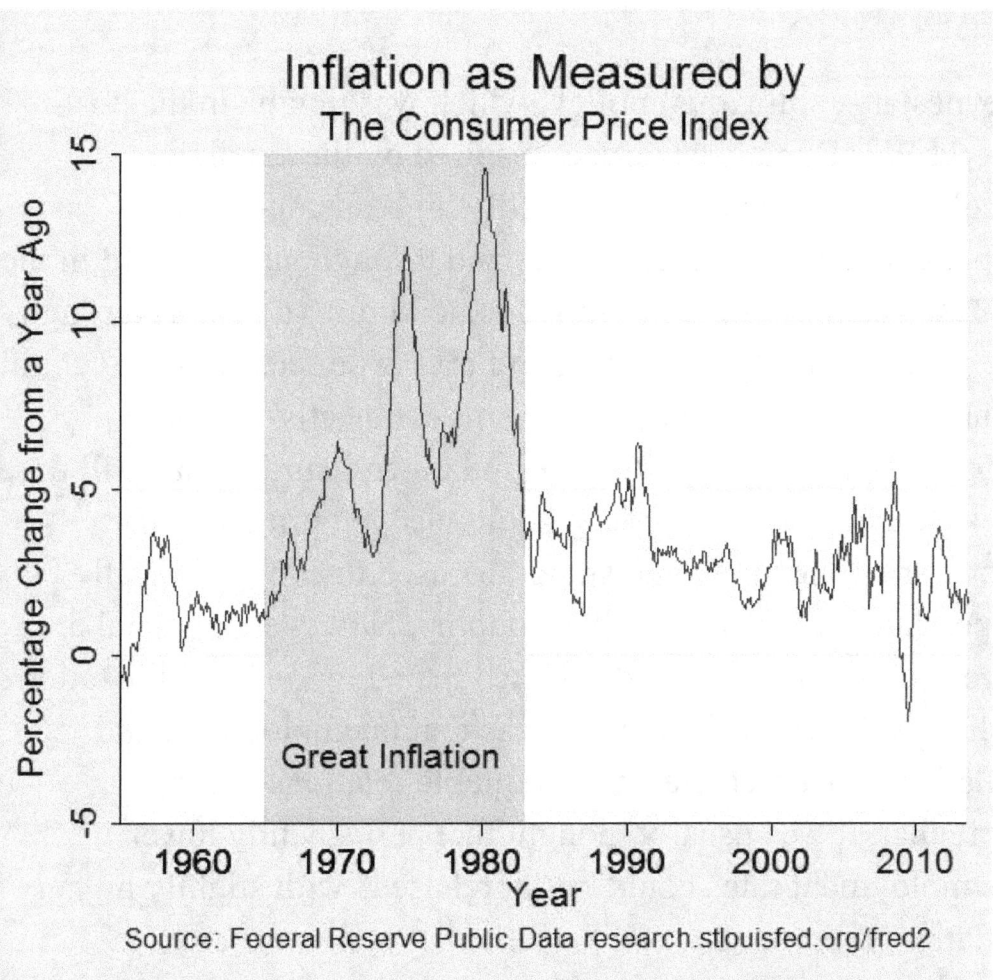

Chart 1: The consumer price index as a measure of inflation. Plotting of data as a curve. Units represent the percentage change from the prior year. The gray bar denotes the Great Inflation, which lasted from January 1965 to December 1982. The consumer price index's annual percentage change started to grow in January 1965 and continued to rise until it reached a peak of over 15% in March 1980. In 1983, the percentage change from the previous year returned to the 0–5% range seen before the Great Inflation. Source: Sam Marshall, Federal Reserve Bank of Richmond; graph produced using data from the Bureau of Labor Statistics via FRED.

Inflation 101

Keynesian stabilization policy, which was dogma in the post-World War II era, was largely inspired by the agonizing recollection of the unprecedentedly high unemployment experienced in the United States and throughout the world in the 1930s. The management of total expenditure (demand) through the fiscal authority's spending and taxing policies and the central bank's monetary policies was the main objective of these programs. The Federal Reserve and other central banks still base their decisions on the widely acknowledged principle that monetary policy may and should be used to control overall expenditure and stabilize the economy. However, a crucial and incorrect premise that underpinned the adoption of stabilization policy in the 1960s and 1970s was that unemployment and inflation had a predictable, exploitable relationship. In particular, it was usually thought that permanently lower unemployment rates could be "purchased" with slightly higher inflation rates.

For policymakers hoping to firmly implement the requirements of the Employment Act, the assumption that the "Phillips curve" represented a longer-term trade-off between inflation, which was occasionally considered to be more of an inconvenience, and unemployment, which was very detrimental to economic well-being, was appealing. 2 The stability of the Phillips curve, however, was a dangerous presumption, and economists Milton Friedman (1968) and Edmund Phelps (1967) issued dire

Inflation 101

warnings against it. According to Phelps, "[i]f the statical 'optimum' is chosen, it is plausible to believe that participants in the labor and product markets will learn to expect inflation...and that, as a result of their logical, anticipatory behavior, the Phillips Curve will progressively shift upward." (1967 Phelps; 1968 Friedman). In other words, the trade-off that policymakers may have wished to pursue between higher inflation and lower unemployment would probably be a false bargain, requiring ever-higher inflation to maintain.

The Instrument: Bretton Woods' Collapse

If the Federal Reserve's policies were firmly rooted, it would not have been possible to chase the Phillips curve in search of reduced unemployment. And thanks to the Bretton Woods pact, the US dollar was inextricably tied to gold in the 1960s. Because of this, the story of the Great Inflation also includes the breakdown of the Bretton Woods system and the detachment of the US currency from its final connection to gold.

The industrialized nations of the globe agreed to a global monetary system during World War II in the hopes that it would increase economic stability and peace by fostering international trade. At Bretton Woods, New Hampshire, in July 1944, forty-four countries came to an agreement on a system that set the exchange rate between the world's currencies and the US dollar and linked the latter to gold.

Inflation 101

But there were a number of implementation issues with the Bretton Woods system, prominent among them the attempt to maintain stable parity between the world's currencies, which was incompatible with their domestic economic objectives. It found out that many countries were pursuing monetary strategies that would march up the Phillips curve towards a more favorable unemployment-inflation nexus.

The US dollar had a further issue because it was the world's reserve currency. Demand for U.S. dollar reserves increased in tandem with the expansion of world trade. An expanding balance of payments deficit temporarily met the demand for US dollars, and as a result, foreign central banks built up larger and larger dollar reserves. Eventually, the amount of dollar reserves held overseas surpassed the US stock of gold, indicating that the US could not sustain full convertibility at the current gold price—a fact that foreign governments and currency speculators would not go unnoticed by.

President Nixon stopped the conversion of US dollars to gold by foreign central banks in the summer of 1971 as inflation began to creep higher throughout the latter half of the 1960s. The short-lived Smithsonian Agreement was an attempt to save the world's monetary system over the course of the following two years, but it failed miserably and quickly disintegrated. The post-World War II global monetary order was over.

The majority of the world's currencies, including the US dollar, were now wholly unanchored as the final connection to gold had been cut. This was the first time in history that the majority of the currencies in the industrialized world were based on an irredeemable paper money standard, with the exception of times of global crisis.

The Opportunity: Fiscal Imbalances, Energy Shortages, and Bad Data

The US economy experienced considerable turbulence during the late 1960s and the early 1970s. At a time when the US financial situation was already stretched by the Vietnam War, President Johnson's Great Society Act resulted in significant spending projects across a wide range of social initiatives. These escalating budget deficits made monetary policy more difficult.

The Federal Reserve adopted a practice of implementing "even-keel" policies in order to prevent monetary policy actions that would conflict with the Treasury's funding plans. This essentially meant that during the time between the announcement of a Treasury issue and its sale to the market, the central bank would maintain its current course of action and hold interest rates stable. Treasury issues were uncommon under normal circumstances, and the Fed's even-keeled policies had little effect on how monetary policy was carried out. However, the Federal Reserve's devotion to the even-keel principle gradually restricted the conduct of monetary policy as debt problems became more prominent (Meltzer 2005).

Inflation 101

The periodic energy crises that raised oil prices and slowed U.S. economy were a more disruptive force. An Arab oil embargo that started in October 1973 and lasted for roughly five months was the first crisis. Crude oil prices quadrupled during this time, reaching a plateau that persisted until a second energy crisis was brought on by the Iranian revolution in 1979. The price of oil tripled during the second crisis.

In the 1970s, economists and decision-makers started to characterize the increase in aggregate prices as various types of inflation. The immediate impact of macroeconomic policy, and specifically monetary policy, was "demand-pull" inflation. It was the outcome of policies that encouraged spending at a higher level than the economy could sustain without exceeding its normal level of productivity and requiring the use of more expensive resources. However, supply interruptions, particularly those originating in the food and energy industries, could also raise inflation (Gordon 1975). 4 Through the chain of production, this "cost-push" inflation also resulted in higher retail prices.

According to the central bank, monetary policy was essentially powerless to stop the inflation brought on by the increase in the price of oil. However, the increase in unemployment brought on by the sharp increase in oil prices was not.

The Federal Reserve allowed significant and rising fiscal imbalances and leaned against the headwinds caused by oil prices since it was mandated to achieve maximum employment with little to no anchor for the management of reserves. Without lowering unemployment, these initiatives increased the money supply and increased total prices.

Policymakers were also hampered by weak data, or at the very least, a poor comprehension of the data. Economist Athanasios Orphanides has demonstrated that when looking back at the data that policymakers had available before and during the Great Inflation, the real-time estimate of potential output was significantly overstated, while the estimate of the rate of unemployment consistent with full employment was significantly underestimated. In other words, officials probably underestimated the effects of their actions on inflation. In actuality, their current course of action couldn't be followed without escalating inflation (Orphanides 1997; Orphanides 2002).

Even worse, the Phillips curve started to fluctuate, whose stability had been a key factor in guiding the Federal Reserve's policy choices.

The Conquest of Us Inflation: From High Inflation to Inflation Targeting

Phelps and Friedman were right. The stable balance between unemployment and inflation turned out to be unstable. Policymakers have a fleeting grasp over any "real" variable.

Inflation 101

This reality also applied to the unemployment rate, which fluctuated about its "natural" rate. There was no trade-off that officials intended to take advantage of.

Any trade-off between inflation and unemployment became a less favorable exchange over time as firms and individuals learned to appreciate, and even anticipate, rising prices. Eventually, both inflation and unemployment reached intolerably high levels. The period that followed was known as "stagflation." When this narrative began in 1964, there was 1% inflation and 5% unemployment. Inflation would reach over 12 percent and unemployment would reach beyond 7 percent ten years later. Inflation was close to 14.5 percent and unemployment was above 7.5 percent during the summer of 1980.

Officials of the Federal Reserve were not unaware of the inflation that was taking place and were fully aware of the dual mandate, which called for the monetary policy to be tuned to achieve both full employment and price stability. In fact, the Full Employment and Balanced Growth Act, sometimes known as the Humphrey-Hawkins Act after the bill's authors, re-codified the Employment Act of 1946 in 1978. Humphrey-Hawkins mandated the Federal Reserve to set goals for the expansion of different monetary aggregates, submit a semiannual Monetary Policy Report to Congress, and achieve full employment and price stability. In spite of this, it seems that when full employment and inflation clashed, the mandate's employment component won out. In the opinion of the public,

Inflation 101

the government, if not also the Federal Reserve, full employment was the top priority, as Fed Chairman Arthur Burns would later claim (Meltzer 2005). But there was also a strong feeling that confronting the inflation issue head-on would have been too expensive for the economy and jobs.

Earlier attempts to reduce inflation without the expensive side effect of increasing unemployment have been made. Between 1971 and 1974, the Nixon government enacted wage and price controls in three stages. The shortages, particularly for food and energy, were made worse by these limitations, which only briefly reduced the rise in prices. In its endeavors, the Ford administration did not do any better. The president launched the Whip Inflation Now (WIN) initiative in 1974 after designating inflation as his "number one adversary," which included voluntary actions to promote greater frugal living. It wasn't successful.

The public had grown accustomed to an inflationary bias in monetary policy by the late 1970s. And they grew more and more dissatisfied with inflation. In the second part of the 1970s, poll after poll revealed that public trust in the economy and government policies was declining. Additionally, inflation was frequently mentioned as a unique evil. Since 1965, it looked like interest rates have been rising secularly. As the 1970s came to an end, they jumped even higher. Business investment decreased, productivity declined, and the country's trade balance with the rest of the globe deteriorated throughout this period.

Inflation 101

And inflation was largely believed to be either the main cause of the economic downturn or to have played a key role in it.

But when both unemployment and inflation reached intolerably high levels, officials were left with a difficult choice. Combating high unemployment would almost surely lead to higher inflation, whereas fighting high inflation would almost certainly lead to higher unemployment.

Former Federal Reserve Bank of New York president Paul Volcker was appointed chairman of the Federal Reserve Board in 1979. Year-over-year inflation was running around 11% when he entered office in August, and the country's unemployment rate was just under 6%. By this time, it was well acknowledged that lowering inflation necessitated tighter control over the rate of reserve expansion in particular and broad money in general. As mandated by the Humphrey-Hawkins Act, the Federal Open Market Committee (FOMC) had already started setting targets for the monetary aggregates. But it was evident that attitudes were changing under the new chairman, and that more drastic steps were needed to restrain the expansion of the money supply. The FOMC said in October 1979 that it would use reserve growth as its primary policy tool rather than the fed funds rate.

Fighting inflation was thus considered essential to achieving both goals of the dual mandate, even if it momentarily disrupted economic activity and, for a while, increased the unemployment rate. Early in 1980, Volcker stated, "[M]y underlying belief is

Inflation 101

that we will eventually have to deal with the inflationary situation since inflation and the unemployment rate tend to coexist over time. Isn't that what the 1970s taught us? (2009) Meltzer (1034).

Even though it wasn't ideal, increased reserve and money growth management over time led to the intended slowdown in inflation. The Monetary Control Act and the implementation of credit controls in the early 1980s also contributed to this tighter reserve management. Interest rates rose throughout 1980, decreased for a short time, and then spiked once more. Between January and July, the lending industry had a decline, unemployment increased, and a brief recession hit the economy. Even when the economy began to improve in the second half of 1980, inflation continued to be high.

The Volcker Fed, however, persisted in its efforts to combat high inflation by combining higher interest rates with even slower reserve growth. In July 1981, the economy experienced another downturn, but this one was more severe and prolonged, lasting until November 1982. While unemployment reached a peak of almost 11 percent, inflation kept falling, and by the time the recession ended, year-over-year inflation had dropped back to less than 5 percent. The Fed's pledge to maintain low inflation gained trust over time, which caused unemployment to decline and the economy to experience sustained growth and stability. The Great Inflation had come to an end.

Inflation 101

Macroeconomic theory had already changed by this point, greatly influenced by the economic lessons of the period. Macroeconomic models now must take into account the crucial part that public expectations play in the interaction between economic policy and economic performance. It has become widely recognized that excellent macroeconomic outcomes depend on making time-consistent policy decisions—decisions that do not trade longer-term prosperity for short-term advantages.

As a result, most central banks, including the Federal Reserve, have established clear numerical inflation targets. Central banks of today recognize that a commitment to price stability is necessary for sound monetary policy. These numerical inflation targets have given monetary policy an anchor once again, to the extent that they are credible. Additionally, they have decreased uncertainty and increased the transparency of monetary policy decisions, which are widely recognized as essential preconditions for achieving long-term growth and maximum employment.

CHAPTER FOUR

THE IMPLICATION OF INFLATION

You might be wondering how all of this inflation discussion affects you. The primary effects of inflation will be discussed in this chapter, but it's crucial to remember that they will vary depending on the rate of inflation. A rate of 2% will not have the same impact as a rate of 100% each year, for example. As a result, we'll examine the repercussions that are predominantly brought on by sustained inflation rates exceeding 2 percent.

NEGATIVE EFFECTS OF INFLATION

1. Money Depreciates in Value

Money loses value as product prices rise. Inflation means that if you save $1 under your pillow for ten years, for instance, you won't be able to buy as much as you could now.

The US dollar has lost more than half of its value between 1980 and 2019, as can be seen by examining its worth during that time period. In other words, a dollar today can buy half the amount of products and services it could have thirty years ago.

Inflation 101

Therefore, if you had $1,000 hidden under your bed in 1980, it would be worth no more than $500.

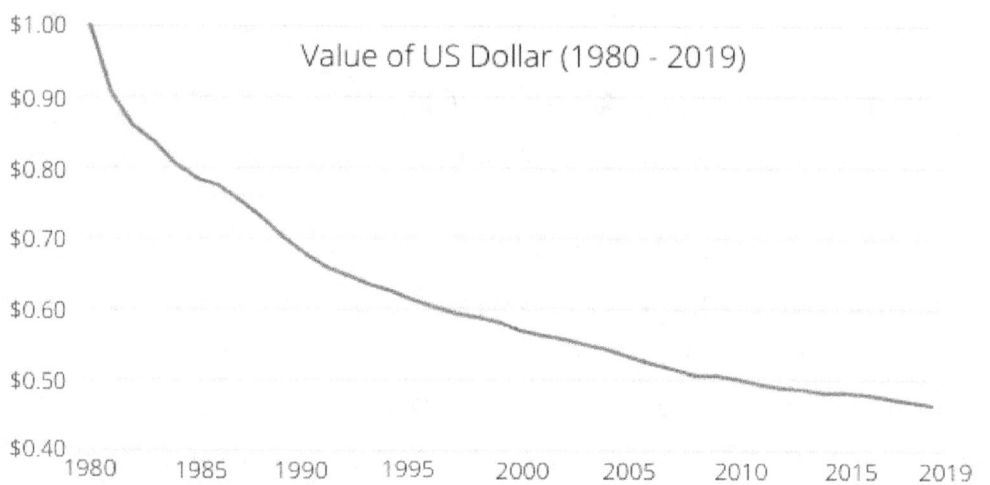

Consumers search for a return on their capital as a result of the loss of purchasing power brought on by inflation. It encourages customers to look for better returns rather than stashing cash beneath the mattress or in low-interest bank accounts. Customers worry that their years of savings would eventually lose all of their value, which is why they behave in this way.

Also, as a result of inflation, businesses are under more pressure to invest any extra cash. Therefore, if money is not being used in some way, it will begin to lose value. Whether this involves investing in stocks or another type of financial instrument.

Inflation 101

2. Inequality

Low-income households are typically hit the most by inflation. Price hikes typically eat up more of their salaries because they spend by far the largest portion of their earnings. For instance, the poor are forced to pay when the cost of necessities like food and housing rises. Someone making $12,000 a year experiences a greater impact from a $10 increase in food prices per week than someone making $50,000.

The tendency for asset prices to increase is one of the repercussions of inflation. Housing, the stock market, and commodities like gold are examples of assets that frequently outperform inflation.

As a result, inequality widens as wealthier people amass more assets. They possess more real estate, stock, and other assets. This means that when inflation happens, the price of these assets rises before the price of common products like bread, milk, eggs, etc. As a result, individuals acquire wealth that enables them to purchase more goods and services than before. Low-income households are also having to spend more money just to get by.

Less money is available for saving and investing in stocks, bonds, and other assets for those with lower salaries since they spend a greater percentage of their income. They are also quite unlikely to be able to afford to invest in large capital purchases like a home. This has the effect of leaving individuals who can

Inflation 101

invest a portion of their income into "inflation protected" assets like stocks in a better position than others.

3. Changes in Exchange Rate

Expanded Money Supply

A nation's currency may depreciate when prices and the money supply rise. If $1 million is in circulation in the US and 30 million YEN are in circulation in China, for instance, this may indicate an exchange rate of 1:30. The ratio will drop to 1:15 if the Federal Reserve adds a further $1 million, bringing the total to $2 million. Given the daily fluctuations in the currency markets, this is only indicative. The fundamental idea is nevertheless the same. Its value relative to other currencies declines as prices rise and the money supply increases.

Let's use another illustration. A Chinese vase costs 100 YEN. With the US, this is exchanged for a barrel of $25 worth of American oil. Based on this transaction, the exchange rate would be 1:4. The price of the vase now stands at YEN 200 due to inflation and increased money printing in China. The vase's value to the US has not increased. Therefore, they wouldn't be ready to exchange two oil barrels for a single vase at the last minute. The currency rate adjusts to the new situation as a result. The exchange rate would increase to 1:8 with the Chinese vase now valued at YEN 200 and the American oil worth $25.

Inflation 101

US Index Comparison of The Weighted Exchange Rate and Inflation

Inflation is Caused by Exchange Rate Decline

The graph above demonstrates that there is a relative relationship between inflation and exchange rate. That does not necessarily imply, though, that fluctuations in the currency rate are a result of inflation. Frequently, additional elements that affect exchange rate swings can cause inflation. In other words, inflation drives a decline in the exchange rate rather than the other way around.

A reduction in the exchange rate can result in cost-push inflation even though an increase in the money supply might cause inflation and the price of a currency to rise. Simply put, this is the situation where imported items cost more because native

Inflation 101

currency can only buy so much. This can be the outcome of a trade deficit, a weak economy, or high interest rates.

4. Effect on Borrowing Costs

If you take out a $200,000 mortgage, you must repay that amount plus interest. There's a chance the it will have a 25-year term and a 5% interest rate. Over $345,000 will be spent over the course of more than 25 years. The expense of only the interest is over $145,000.

The actual cost is $205,000 when inflation from the last 25 years (1995-2020) is taken into account. In other words, the $345,000 total cost is equivalent to $205,000 at 1995 values in 2020. Inflation can thus lower the cost even though we are staring at an exorbitant amount of money to repay.

To put it another way, the initial borrowed funds lose value over time. As a result, the debtor is required to provide fewer resources to repay the obligation. For instance, a debtor might make $20,000 after taxes each year. Additionally, they take out a loan for $40,000, which is equal to two years' worth of pay. But after five years, inflation increased their pay to the point where it was equal to one year's salary, or $40,000.

Having said that, persistently high inflation may force financial institutions to raise their interest rates in order to defend against inflationary pressures. Therefore, borrowers can actually find it more difficult to get credit.

Inflation 101

5. Increasing Cost of Living

It goes without saying that consumers will pay more when the cost of items rises in order to purchase both essentials and luxuries. If incomes increase in accordance with inflation, this might not necessarily be a problem, but those who don't will see increased actual prices. Or, to put it another way, they will have to spend a larger proportion of their income on the same amount of goods.

Inflation also causes tax payers to move into higher tax brackets, which results in some paying higher taxes. The brackets suffer if the new reality is not sufficiently taken into account.

Low skilled workers are particularly impacted because of how sticky their earnings are as a result of the intense market rivalry. Due to the high competition for jobs among low-skilled individuals, businesses are in a powerful position. To make matters worse, earnings can lag behind the rest of the economy. Additionally, minimum wage increases may not always coincide with inflation, which further depresses income.

Inflation 101

POSITIVE EFFECTS OF INFLATION

1. Increased Investment and Spending

Consumers are encouraged to make purchases as the inflation rate rises. Consumers sensibly decide to buy now rather than pay more next year rather than wait till the goods is more expensive.

This entails buying brand-new automobiles, refrigerators, phones, and other consumer goods for the typical consumer. However, this goes beyond simple consumer items. The best return on investment is another incentive for consumers. Money must be "beat" in order to keep its purchasing power constant as it begins to lose value due to inflation.

For instance, a customer might have $1,000 in the bank earning only 1% interest. However, if inflation remains at 3% year after year, they will be losing money. They can then respond in one of two ways.

Let inflation first take hold and watch their currency lose value. Or, secondly, look for investments with larger yields. Savings are being directed toward sectors of the economy that will be most productive, which is good for the economy.

This, however, poses a risk because it's possible that the typical consumer lacks the expertise or understanding needed to make a smart investment. Consequently, there is a higher chance of financial loss as a result of bad money management.

Inflation 101

2. Increasing Asset Prices

In the past, asset prices have risen faster than inflation. For instance, typically, long-term property values have exceeded inflation. In 1980, the average price of a home sold in the US was $74,500; now, that same home would be worth $231,000 after inflation. In contrast, the typical home now sells for $375,000, representing enormous real gains of $144,000 over a period of 39 years.

Another excellent illustration is the stock market. The S&P 500 has generated returns of 10% annually on average since its inception in 1926. It returns a rate that is more than 7% above inflation once we adjust for inflation.

Consumers and organizations move forward with their purchase decisions and spend more quickly during periods of continuous inflation. Alternately, they invest their money in less liquid assets like stocks, bonds, and real estate. In actuality, both of these things occur.

3. Lowers Effective Debt Level

Whether it's a company, the government, or the consumer, people who are heavily indebted may actually profit from higher inflation rates. The borrower's debt, for instance, can have a 2% interest rate. Their effective rate of repayment will decrease if inflation is 10% and their income increases at a similar amount.

For those who are in debt, this may be a benefit of inflation, but for savers and other persons and organizations, such as banks, it may really be a significant negative. Banks suffer as a result of their interest rates being below the rate of inflation. Additionally, savers are probably earning interest that is less than the rate of inflation.

4. It Is Preferable to Deflation.

Numerous economists debate whether a rate of inflation of 1%, 2%, or 4% is the best one. It is generally agreed upon, though, that whatever it is, it is generally preferable to deflation.

Perhaps deflation is worse for an economy than inflation. It might make it more difficult for both governments for private companies and people to pay off their debts. As a result, public services may virtually be paralyzed, and a significant number of businesses may file for bankruptcy because they are unable to make payments that are essentially growing more expensive.

CHAPTER FIVE

HOW TO BEAT INFLATION

Even though you may not be able to prevent inflation, you can plan for it. Money kept in cash or low-APY bank accounts will eventually lose purchasing power, even at a mild pace of inflation. By investing your money in particular assets, you can reduce inflation and increase your purchasing power.

Invest in Stocks to Beat Inflation

One approach to perhaps fight inflation is to make stock market investments. While individual stock prices may decline, businesses may fail, and indices may even experience temporary declines during bad markets, overall stock market indices improve over time, outpacing inflation.

The S&P 500, which monitors the performance of 500 of the biggest U.S. corporations, generated an average annual return of little over 10% from 1920 to 2020, with dividends reinvested. This represents a long-term average; the S&P 500 has occasionally experienced lower or even negative returns.

There are no assurances when investing in individual equities, but a well-diversified investment in a wide market index fund

Inflation 101

can increase wealth over many years and outperform inflation. Investments in S&P 500 index funds have generated over 6% returns annually on average between June 1930 and June 2020, even after accounting for inflation.

Invest in Bonds to Beat Inflation

Bonds typically provide lower returns than stocks, but they can outperform inflation. The more reliable returns of investing in bonds and bond funds may appeal to risk-averse investors or those nearing or in retirement who want to outpace inflation.

The Bloomberg Barclays U.S. Aggregate Bond Index, a benchmark index that tracks thousands of U.S. bonds, saw annual returns of 4.47% from June 2005 to June 2020. Those who had money invested in bonds would have enjoyed small increases in their money's purchasing power even after accounting for inflation. But keep in mind that bond yields are influenced by the state of the economy as a whole, and that they can be considerably lower now than they were in the past.

Treasury Security Protected Against Inflation (TIPS)

A unique type of U.S. treasury bonds called Treasury Inflation-Protected Securities (TIPS) is made with the goal of shielding investors from inflation. TIPS automatically raises the value of your bond in line with inflation by adjusting the value of your investment in accordance with changes to the CPI. TIPS pay

Inflation 101

interest during the course of the bond's five-, ten-, or thirty-year tenure.

Can Gold Help You Beat Inflation?

Although there is still considerable disagreement on this claim, many investors believe gold to be the best inflation hedge.

For instance, the price of gold climbed by 7.6% year on average between April 1968 and June 2020. Returns average 3.6% after inflation adjustment. However, gold's value fell by 28% and 12%, respectively, in 2013 and 2015, indicating that it is not the reliable safe haven some believe it to be.

This is due to the fact that the price of gold can fluctuate greatly over time and is influenced by changes in the value of other currencies, decisions made by the Fed and other central banks regarding monetary policy, as well as irregular supply and demand.

Additionally, investing in gold has a special set of difficulties. If you purchase gold, you must locate a safe place to store it, which has additional charges. Gold is subject to a higher long-term capital gains tax rate than stocks and bonds when sold after being held for a year or more.

CHAPTER SIX

CONCLUSION

Despite the fact that the recent jump in consumer goods inflation does not indicate that this sector will experience persistent inflation in the future, the recent increases in house prices and the labor supply and demand in the services sector both pose risks to the inflation forecast.

The need for labor in the services industry will increase beyond existing high levels as consumer spending rebalances towards services. For instance, employment was 1.5 million below its pre-pandemic level in September but job postings in leisure and hospitality were a startling 530,000 higher than average. The need for labor will probably grow dramatically if consumer demand for leisure and hospitality services returns to (or briefly exceeds) pre-pandemic levels.

Concerns about a shortage of workers have been highlighted by softening labor force participation rates and a frustratingly slow pace of matching job seekers with jobs. The sheer volume of job vacancies and prospects across numerous industries that candidates must take into account undoubtedly slows the pace of job matching. Additionally, some people are unable to work or

Inflation 101

are concerned about the health dangers of working due to pandemic-related difficulties. I believe such problems will be resolved.

The experience of the pandemic and the evolving character of work since March 2020 may, however, continuously depress how much labor people are willing to offer, according to prolonged weakening in the labor supply. The capacity of the US economy to generate goods and services will be hampered if the labor supply remains constrained. For a certain level of aggregate demand, that would lead to an increase in inflationary pressures, which is undesirable. However, since our standard of living would be lower, that would be the issue that needed to be addressed most.

The rise in housing prices and how it will affect the rental market are the other factors that are posing some inflationary threats in the near future. Inflation in the rental market has a strong historical correlation with house price rise (figure 5). Before the pandemic, rents climbed at a rate of over 334 percent annually, but in the first half of this year, the inflation rate was astonishingly low at less than 2 percent. Rent inflation has now reached more normal levels; between October 2020 and October 2021, rentals increased by 234 percent, and it appears that this rate will continue to rise. Even if it is noteworthy, the inflation in this area would be more of the unremarkable variety, which a less accommodating monetary policy would be well-suited to temper.

Inflation 101

The forces currently at play in the goods sector will not persist, so this is not the biggest risk to inflation in the future. The main danger is that there won't be enough labor available to meet the large growth in demand for workers in the services industry.

By keeping the pandemic under control with immunizations and prudent health policies, policymakers can promote labor supply. Additionally, authorities can eliminate obstacles that make working expensive, like a lack of access to reasonably priced, high-quality childcare. By improving access to information about the labor market and organizing job fairs, policymakers can help match job searchers with employers. Finally, immigrants are a crucial source of employees for the United States, albeit they are now arriving at considerably lower rates than were anticipated before the pandemic. Returning to more normal levels of, say, green card issuance would aid in increasing the labor supply in the US to meet the rising labor demand. In other words, the same policies that support a prolonged and equitable labor market recovery also support future efforts to control inflation.